BRANCH LINES
TO
MONMOUTH

Vic Mitchell and Keith Smith

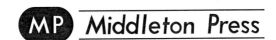

MP Middleton Press

Front cover: Standing at the hub of the system on 15th August 1957 is 0-4-2T no. 1456. It is waiting to start its journey with the 12.45pm Monmouth (Troy) to Ross-on-Wye autocoach. (P.Q.Treloar coll.)

Back cover: The goods shed at Coleford forms the nucleus of Coleford Railway Museum, which records the diverse aspects of operating the local routes in a bygone age. (P.G.Barnes)

Published January 2008
First reprint August 2012

ISBN 978 1 906008 20 8

© Middleton Press, 2008

Design Deborah Esher

Typesetting Barbara Mitchell

Published by
     Middleton Press
     Easebourne Lane
     Midhurst
     West Sussex
     GU29 9AZ
Tel: 01730 813169
Fax: 01730 812601
Email: info@middletonpress.co.uk
www.middletonpress.co.uk

Printed in the United Kingdom by IJ Graphics, Guildford, Surrey. GU2 9XW

CONTENTS

INDEX

ACKNOWLEDGEMENTS

We are very grateful for the assistance received from many of those mentioned in the credits also to A.R.Carder, L.Crosier, G.Croughton, F.Hornby, J.B.Horne, S.C.Jenkins, N.Langridge, B.Lewis, I.Pope, Mr D. and Dr S.Salter and, in particular, our always supportive wives, Barbara Mitchell and Janet Smith.

I. Railway Clearing House map for 1947, with the 1883-1917 Coleford branch from Monmouth added.

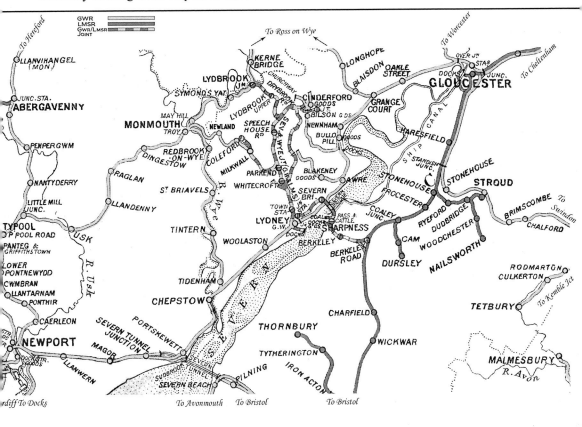

GEOGRAPHICAL SETTING

Pontypool Road station is situated near the watershed of the River Usk and the Afon Llwyd. The route to Monmouth dropped into the valley of the former at the town of Usk. It crossed the river near the station and then climbed gently, close to a small tributary called the Olway Brook. The summit was reached east of Raglan and a steady descent followed to Monmouth alongside the River Troddi.

The Wye Valley Branch diverged from the South Wales main line east of Chepstow and climbed steeply to a tunnel through a headland formed by one of the major meanders of the River Wye, which has deeply incised the Limestone of this area. Thereafter, the railway followed a winding course close to the Wye, one further tunnel being necessary south of Tintern.

Monmouth was the county town and two major bridges were required south of it to carry the Chepstow and the Ross lines over the Wye. The latter route ran close to this river to Lydbrook Junction, although a larger meander was avoided by a short tunnel at Symonds Yat. This section, together with the Usk-Monmouth length, ran mainly on Lower Old Red Sandstone.

The Wye Valley line ran in both Monmouthshire and Gloucestershire, as the boundary of the counties was in the River Wye, south of Redbrook. The other routes were mostly in the former county, although the eastern two stations were in the latter.

The maps are to the scale of 25ins to 1 mile, with north at the top unless otherwise indicated.

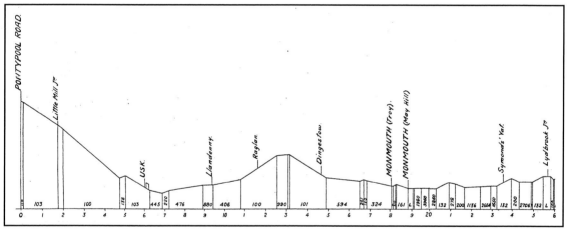

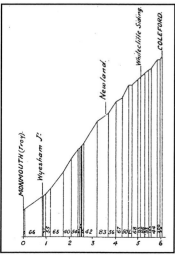

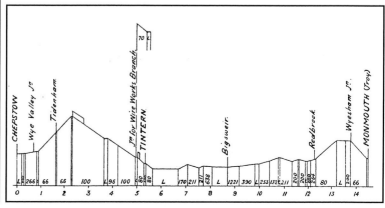

Gradient Profiles.

HISTORICAL BACKGROUND

The first line in the area was the South Wales Railway, which opened from Gloucester to the east bank of the River Wye at Chepstow in 1851.

The Newport, Abergavenny & Hereford Railway of 1853 and the 1855 Hereford, Ross & Gloucester Railway completed a triangle in which our lines were built. The triangle became part of the Great Western Railway.

The Coleford, Monmouth, Usk & Pontypool Railway was authorised under an Act of 1853 and opened between Little Mill and Usk on 2nd June 1856. It was operated by the NAHR until 12th October 1857, when the line was extended to Monmouth. The branch was worked by the West Midland Railway from that date, trains terminating at Pontypool Road, with Little Mill Junction closing. (It reopened in 1863.)

The Ross & Monmouth Railway opened on 4th August 1873; it was built under an Act of 1865. However, there was a gap between the two Monmouth stations, due to bridge construction, until 1st May 1874. The Ross & Monmouth Railway was nominally independent until 1922, although the GWR operated the trains. The Severn & Wye Railway linked the valleys in its title and reached Lydbrook Junction in 1874.

The Act for the Wye Valley Railway was passed in August 1866 and trains began running between Chepstow and Monmouth on 1st November 1876. A branch from it to Coleford was opened by the Coleford Railway on 1st September 1883. This became part of the GWR in 1884, the CMUPR following in 1887, the WVR in 1905 and the RMR in 1922.

The Monmouth-Coleford passenger service was withdrawn on 1st January 1917 and the western part of the branch was closed completely. Passenger traffic between Lydbrook Junction and Lydney Town ceased on 8th July 1929.

The GWR became the Western Region of British Railways upon nationalisation in 1948 and passenger services to Monmouth were withdrawn thus: from Pontypool Road on 13th June 1955 and from Chepstow and Ross-on-Wye on 5th January 1959. The Hereford-Gloucester route followed on 2nd November 1964.

Freight continued west of Usk until 1965 and to Glascoed until 1993. Such trains ran north of Tintern until 1964 and south thereof until 1986. The Ross-on-Wye to Lydbrook Junction section carried a little freight until 1964. Details are given in the captions.

PASSENGER SERVICES

From Pontypool Road
In the 19th century, there were three or four trains on weekdays, with one on Sundays in some of the early years. In the 20th century, five trips were common, with some running through to Ross-on-Wye. However, Sunday trains were run mainly in the late 1930s, when there were usually two. In this period, there were often six on weekdays. There was a reduction to three during part of World War II, when one or two extras terminated at Usk. A remarkable increase to eleven weekday trains took place on 14th June 1954, but the end was nigh.

From Chepstow
Four weekday trains was the norm for most of the life of the line; some Sunday trains ran between the wars. The final timetable from 23rd May 1955 included an extra train in the evenings.

From Lydbrook Junction and Ross-on-Wye
Five trains appeared in most weekday timetables; Sunday services were limited mainly to the period prior to World War II, when there were often two trips.

Coleford Branch
For most of its short life, this six mile long route had four trains, weekdays only.

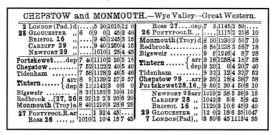

CHEPSTOW and MONMOUTH.—Wye Valley—Great Western.

July 1878

WYE VALLEY and COLEFORD LINES.—Great Western.

January 1901

b Except Sunday nights. * Great Western Station. † Temple Meads.

PONTYPOOL ROAD, MONMOUTH, and ROSS.—Great Western.

January 1901

b Arrives at 7 52 mrn. * Panteg and Griffithstown. † Station for Goodrich Castle.

SEVERN TUNNEL, CHEPSTOW, MONMOUTH, and COLEFORD.—Great Western.

June 1920

SERVICE SUSPENDED.

ROSS, MONMOUTH, and PONTYPOOL ROAD.—Great Western.

June 1920

SEVERN TUNNEL, CHEPSTOW, and MONMOUTH—(One class only)

August 1940

¶ "Halts" at Caldicot, between Severn Tunnel Junc. & Portskewett, at Tutshill (for Beachley), between Chepstow & Tidenham, at Netherhope, between Tidenham & Tintern, at Brockweir and at Llandogo, between Tintern & St. Briavels, at Whitebrook and at Penallt, between St. Briavels and Redbrook-on-Wye, and at Wyesham, between Redbrook-on-Wye and Monmouth (Troy).

August 1940

ROSS-ON-WYE, MONMOUTH, and PONTYPOOL ROAD—(One class only)

Miles	Down.	Week Days only.																				
		mrn	mrn		mrn		mrn	mrn		mrn	mrn Saturdays only.		aft Saturdays only.	aft		aft	aft Except Saturdays.		aft	aft		aft
	Ross-on-Wye ¶ ....dep.	..	7 13	..	..	..	8 22	..	..	11 0	1146	..	..	3 5	..	..	4 30	..	5 10	..	..	7 25
4	Kerne Bridge A........	..	7 23	..	..	..	8 32	..	..	1110	1156	..	..	3 15	..	..	4 40	..	5 20	..	..	7 35
5½	Lydbrook Junction	..	7 26	..	..	..	8 36	..	..	1114	1159	..		3 19	..	..	4 44	..	5 24	..	..	7 39
7½	Symonds Yat........	..	..	..	..	..	8 41	..	..	1119		..		3 24	..	..		..	5 29	..	..	7 44
12½	Monmouth (May Hill)........	..	..	..	..	..	8 50	..	..	1129		..		3 34	..	..		..	5 38	..	..	7 53
13	" (Troy) 89.. arr.	..	..	..	..	..	8 55	..	..	1131		..		3 37	..	..		..	5 42	..	..	7 58
	dep.	7 28	..	..	..	..	..	9 15	..	..		..		..	..	3 51		..	..	7 5	..	..
16½	Dingestow ¶........	7 34	..	..	..	..	..	9 21	..	..		..		..	..	3 57		..	..	7 11	..	..
19½	Raglan ¶........	7 42	..	..	..	..	..	9 30	..	..		..		..	..	4 6		..	..	7 20	..	..
21¾	Llandenny........	7 49	..	..	..	..	..	9 37	..	..		..		..	..	4 13		..	..	7 27	..	..
25	Usk	7 57	..	..	8 50	..	..	9 45	..	..		..	1 50	..	..	4 21		..	..	7 35	..	..
27	Glascoed Halt........[125	8 2	..	..	8 55	..	..	9 51	..	..		..	1 55	..	..	4 27	..	..	..	7 41	..	..
29	Little Mill Junction ..[122,	8 7	..	..	8 58	..	..	9 56	..	..	..	..	1 59	..	..	4 32	..	..	..	7 46	..	..
31	Pontypool Road 80, arr.	8 11	..	..	9 3	..	..	10 2	..	..	..	..	2 4	..	..	4 38	..	..	..	7 52	..	..

Miles	Up.	Week Days only.																				
		mrn	mrn		mrn		mrn		aft Saturdays only.	aft		aft Saturdays only.	aft		aft	aft		aft Except Saturdays.	aft		aft	aft
	Pontypool Road........dep.	..	7 42	..	8 33	..	..	..		..	..	1 25	2 30	..	..	3 54	..	..	..	..	6 5	..
2	Little Mill Junction........	..	7 46	..	8 37	..	..	..		..	..	1 34	2 34	..	..	4 0	..	..	..	..	6 10	..
4	Glascoed Halt........	..	7 50	..	8 41	..	..	..		..	..	1 38	2 38	..	..	4 4	..	..	..	..	6 15	..
6	Usk	..	7 59	..	8 47	..	..	..		..	..	1 44	2 44	..	..	4 10	..		..	..	6 21	..
9¼	Llandenny ¶........	..	8 6	..	..	..	..	..		..	..		2 51	..	..	..	..		..	..	6 28	..
11½	Raglan ¶........	..	8 12	..	..	..	..	..		..	..		2 57	..	..	..	..		..	..	6 36	..
14½	Dingestow........	..	8 21	..	..	..	..	..		..	..		3 5	..	..	..	..		..	..	6 47	..
18	Monmouth (Troy) 89.. arr.	..	8 26	..	..	..	..	..		..	..		3 12	..	..	..	..		..	..	6 53	..
	dep.	..	8A28	..	..	..	9 36	..		1 5	..		..	..	3 51	..	..		6 5	..	..	8 23
18½	" (May Hill)........	..	8A30	..	..	..	9 40	..		1 9	..		..	..	3 54	..	..		6 9	..	..	8 27
23½	Symonds' Yat........	..	..	..	..	..	9 50	..		1 19	..		..	..	4 4	..	..		6 19	..	..	8 37
25½	Lydbrook Junction	7 42	..	..	..	..	9 57	..	1210	1 25	..		..	..	4 9	..	..	4 50	6 24	..	..	8 42
27	Kerne Bridge A ¶........	7 46	..	..	..	..	10 1	..	1214	1 29	..	..	..	..	4 13	..	..	4 54	6 28	..	..	8 46
31	Ross-on-Wye (below)....arr.	7 55	..	..	..	..	1010	..	1223	1 38	..	..	..	..	4 22	..	..	5 3	6 37	..	..	8 57

A Station for Goodrich Castle. A Not during School Holidays.

¶ "Halts" at Walford between Ross-on-Wye and Kerne Bridge; at Elms Bridge, between Dingestow and Raglan and at Raglan Road Crossing between Raglan and Llandenny.

January 1955

SEVERN TUNNEL, CHEPSTOW, and MONMOUTH
(Third class only, limited accommodation)

Miles		Week Days only					
		a.m	a.m		p.m	p.m	p.m Commences 23rd May
	104 Newport........dep	7B5	9B40	..	1B40	4F10	6F5
—	Severn Tunnel Junc. "	7B30	10B1	..	2B1	5 0	7 10
1	Caldicot Halt....... "	7B32	10B3	..	2B3	5 3	7 12
2¾	Portskewett .... "	7B38	10B8	..	2B7	5 7	7 16
7½	Chepstow .... "	7 55	10 40	..	2 35	5 16	7 25
8	Tutshill Halt (for Beach-	7 57	10 42	..	2 37	5 19	7 28
8¾	Tidenham Halt ....(ley)	8 3	10 49	..	2 43	5 24	7 33
9½	Netherhope Halt	8 6	10 51	..	2 45	5 26	7 35
12¾	Tintern........	8 14	10 59	..	2 53	5 34	7 43
13	Brockweir Halt........	8 15	11 1	..	2 55	5 35	7 45
15¼	Llandogo Halt........	8 20	11 6	..	2 59	5 39	7 49
16¼	St. Briavels........	8 23	11 10	..	3 2	5 42	7 52
17½	Whitebrook Halt........	8 27	11 14	..	3 6	5 46	7 56
19¼	Penallt Halt........	8 31	11 19	..	3 10	5 50	8 0
19½	Redbrook-on-Wye........	8 34	11 20	..	3 12	5 52	8 3
21¼	Wyesham Halt	8 39	11 25	..	3 17	5 57	8 8
21½	Monmouth (Troy) ¶ arr	8 43	11 29	..	3 21	6 1	8 10

Mls		Week Days only				
		a.m	a.m	p.m	p.m	p.m Commences 23rd May
—	Monmouth (Troy) ¶ dep	9 0	11 40	3 55	6 6	8 15
¼	Wyesham Halt	9 2	11 42	3 56	6 8	8 17
2¼	Redbrook-on-Wye........	9 7	11 47	4 1	6 13	8 22
2½	Penallt Halt........	9 8	11 49	4 3	6 14	8 24
4¼	Whitebrook Halt........	9 13	11 53	4 7	6 19	8 28
5¼	St. Briavels........	9 17	11 57	4 11	6 23	8 32
6¼	Llandogo Halt........	9 20	12 0	4 16	6 26	8 35
8¾	Brockweir Halt........	9 24	12 4	4 21	6 30	8 39
9	Tintern........	9 26	12 6	4 23	6 33	8 42
12¼	Netherhope Halt	9 35	12 14	4 32	6 41	8 50
13	Tidenham Halt ....(ley)	9 37	12 16	4 34	6 44	8 53
13¾	Tutshill Halt (for Beach-	9 42	12 20	4 38	6 49	8 56
14¼	Chepstow .... arr	9 45	12 23	4 40	6 51	8 58
19	Portskewett........ "	10B9	12 32	4 49	7B14	9B22
20¾	Caldicot Halt....... "	10B13	12 36	4 53	..	9B33
21¾	Severn Tunnel Junc. "	10B15	12 38	4 55	7 3	9B28
31¾	104 Newport........ "	10B38	1 0	5F38	7F44	9B46

B Change at Chepstow F Change at Severn Tunnel Junction ¶ Bus Services operate between: Ross-on-Wye and Coleford; Coleford and Lydney; Coleford and Monmouth; and Coleford & Lydbrook

January 1955

ROSS-ON-WYE, MONMOUTH, and PONTYPOOL ROAD—(Third class only)

Miles		Week Days only																			
		a.m	a.m	a.m	a.m	a.m	a.m	a.m		p.m	p.m	p.m	p.m	p.m	p.m Except Saturdays	p.m	p.m	p.m	p.m Commences 28th May	p.m	p.m
	Ross-on-Wye ¶........ dep	7 5	C	8 15	A	A	11 0	A	..	..	A	3 0	..	..	4 30	5 15	..	..	7 0	..	F
3½	Walford Halt........	7 12	..	8 22	..	..	11 6	..	..	..	..	3 6	..	..	4 37	5 21	..	..	7 6	..	..
4	Kerne Bridge	7 14	..	8 25	..	..	11 9	..	..	..	..	3 9	..	..	4 40	5 24	..	..	7 9	..	..
5½	Lydbrook Junction........	7 18	..	8K34	..	..	11 13	..	..	..	..	3 13	..	..	4 43	5 28	..	..	7 13	..	..
7½	Symonds Yat........	..	..	8 39	..	..	11 18	..	..	..	..	3 18	..	..		5 33	..	..	7 18	..	..
—	Hadnock Halt	..	..	8A44	..	..	11A25	..	..	..	..	3A25	X	..		5A40	..	..	7A25	..	..
12½	Monmouth (May Hill)........	..	..	8 50	..	..	11 30	..	..	..	..	3 28	3 45	..		5 43	..	..	7 27	..	..
13	" (Troy) ¶.... arr	..	X	8 53	X	X	11 34	X	..	X	X	3 31	3 47	X		5 47	X	X	7 32	X	X
	dep	..	7 35	..	9 0	1043	..	11 48	..	1245	1 50	..	3 48	4 55		..	6 5	7 5		8 45	10 15
16½	Dingestow........	..	7 40	..	9 5	1048	..	11 53	..	1250	1 55	..	3 53	5 0		..	6 10	7 10		8 50	..
18¾	Elms Bridge Halt........	..	..	..	9 10	..	..	..	..	..	..	..	3 59	..		..	..	..		8 56	..
19½	Raglan	..	7 48	..	9 12	1055	..	12 1	..	1256	2 3	..	4 1	5 8		..	6 18	7 18		8 58	10 28
20¾	Raglan Rd. Crossing Halt ..	..	7 51	..	9 15	1058	..	12 4	..	..	2 6	..	4 4	5 11	..	..	6 21	7 21		9 1	..
21¾	Llandenny	..	7 53	..	9 17	11 0	..	12 6	..	1 0	2 8	..	4 6	5 13	..	..	6 23	7 23		9 3	10 34
—	Cefntilla Halt	..	7 55	..	9 20	11 3	..	12 8	..	..	2 10	..	4 8	5 15	..	..	6 26	7 25		9 5	10 35
25	Usk	..	8 2	..	9 24	1110	..	12 14	..	1 6	2 14	..	4 13	5 25	..	..	6 29	7 30		9 10	10 41
27	Glascoed Halt	..	8 9	..	9 29	1115	..	12 19	..	..	2 19	..	4 18	5 30	..	..	6 35	7 34	..	9 15	..
29	Little Mill Junction Halt ..	..	8 11	..	9 33	1119	..	12 23	..	1 15	2 23	..	4 22	5 34	..	..	6 39	7 38	..	9 19	..
31	Pontypool Road........ arr	..	8 17	..	9 38	1125	..	12 28	..	1 20	2 28	..	4 26	5 40	..	..	6 45	7 45	..	9 23	10 53

Mls		a.m	a.m	a.m	a.m	a.m	a.m	a.m		p.m	p.m	p.m	p.m	p.m	p.m Except Saturdays	p.m	p.m	p.m	p.m Commences 28th May	p.m	F
	Pontypool Road........dep	6 45	..	7 46	..	9 55	10 50	11 55	..	..	12 50	2 30	..	3 44	..	5 10	..	6 10	..	7 55	9 28
2	Little Mill Junction Halt ..	6 49	..	7 50	..	9 59	10 55	12 0	..	..	12 55	2 34	..	3 49	..	5 14	..	6 14	..	7 59	..
5	Glascoed Halt........	..	..	7 54	..	10 3	10 59	12 4	..	..	12 59	2 38	..	3 53	..	5 18	..	6 18	..	8 3	..
6	Usk	6 58	..	8 3	..	10 10	11 6	12 12	..	..	1 8	2 45	..	4 13	..	5 23	..	6 30		8 10	9 40
—	Cefntilla Halt	7 2	..	8 6	..	10 15	11 13	12 17	..	..	1 12	2 48	..	4 18	..	5 27	..	6 35		8 14	9 44
9¼	Llandenny	7 5	..	8 10	..	10 17	11 16	12 20	..	..	1 15	2 52	..	4 20	..	5 30	..	6 39		8 19	9 47
10¼	Raglan Rd. Crossing Halt ..	7 8	..	8 13	..	10 20	11 19	12 22	..	..	1 17	2 55	..	4 22	..	5 33	..	6Y42		8 21	9Y50
11½	Raglan	7 11	..	8 16	..	10 23	11 21	12 25	..	..	1 20	2 58	..	4 25		5 36	..	6 45		8 24	9 53
12¼	Elms Bridge Halt	..	..	8 19	..	..	11 25	12 28	..	..	1 23	..	..	4 28		5 39	..	6Y48		8 27	..
14½	Dingestow........	7 19	..	8 25	..	10 31	11 31	12 34	..	..	1 29	3 6	..	4 34		5 43	..	6Y54		8 33	10Y1
18	Monmouth (Troy) ¶.... arr	7 24	..	8 31	..	10 37	11 36	12 40	..	..	1 37	3 12	..	4 40		5 52	..	7 0		8 40	10 8
	dep	X	..	X	9 36	X	X	X	..	12 50	X	3 35	3 51	X		X	6 5	X	8 25	X	X
18½	" (May Hill)	A	..	A	9 39	A	C	A	..	12 53	A	3 37	3 54	..		..	6 8	..	8 28	..	C
—	Hadnock Halt	..	..	..	9A42	..	..	..	..	12A55	..	X	3A56	..		..	6A10	..	8A30	..	..
23½	Symonds Yat........	..	..	..	9 50	..	..	..	..	1 3	..	..	4 4	..		..	6 18	..	8 38	..	..
25½	Lydbrook Junction........	..	7 35	..	9 55	..	..	..	..	1 8	..	..	4 9	..	4 55	..	6 24	..	8 44	..	..
27	Kerne Bridge	..	7 38	..	10 0	..	..	..	..	1 12	..	..	4 13	..	4 59	..	6 28	..	8 48	..	..
27½	Walford Halt........	..	7 41	..	10 3	..	..	..	..	1 15	..	..	4 16	..	5 2	..	6 32	..	8 53	..	..
31	Ross-on-Wye ¶........arr	..	7 48	..	1010	..	..	..	..	1 22	..	..	4 23	..	5 8	..	6 39	..	9 0	..	..

A To and from Pontypool (Clarence St.) (Table 137) A Calls to take up or set down. Passengers wishing to alight must give notice to the Guard at the previous *stopping* station and those desiring to join should give the necessary hand signal to the Driver. C To and from Newport (Table 165) F Thurdays and Saturdays K Arr. 8 30 a.m. X Limited accommodation
Y Calls to set down on notice being given to the Guard at Usk

¶ Bus services operate between: Ross-on-Wye and Coleford; Coleford and Lydney; Coleford and Monmouth; and Coleford and Lydbrook

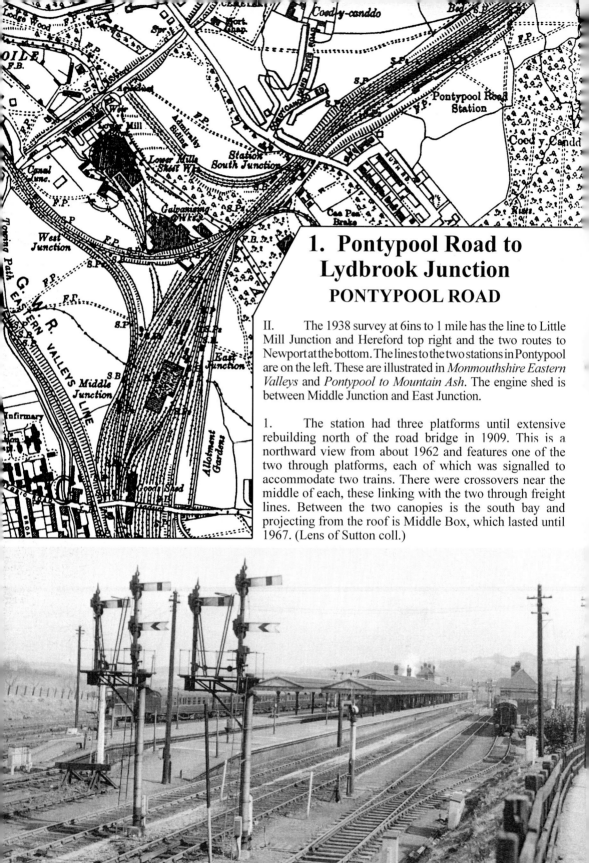

1. Pontypool Road to Lydbrook Junction
PONTYPOOL ROAD

II.   The 1938 survey at 6ins to 1 mile has the line to Little Mill Junction and Hereford top right and the two routes to Newport at the bottom. The lines to the two stations in Pontypool are on the left. These are illustrated in *Monmouthshire Eastern Valleys* and *Pontypool to Mountain Ash*. The engine shed is between Middle Junction and East Junction.

1.   The station had three platforms until extensive rebuilding north of the road bridge in 1909. This is a northward view from about 1962 and features one of the two through platforms, each of which was signalled to accommodate two trains. There were crossovers near the middle of each, these linking with the two through freight lines. Between the two canopies is the south bay and projecting from the roof is Middle Box, which lasted until 1967. (Lens of Sutton coll.)

2.   We take a closer look at the same platform in May 1962 and see the scissors crossover more clearly. To the right of it are carriage sidings. (Nelson coll./T.Walsh)

3.   The north bay was termed platform 4 and is seen on 12th October 1957 with this commemorative special. The bay was normally used by trains for Monmouth, which were often formed of GWR diesel railcars from 1936 onwards. (G.Adams/M.J.Stretton coll.)

4.   Staffing ceased here in 1971 and four southbound freight trains were recorded on 23rd June 1979. North Box had been in the distance until 1973; South Box was on a site behind the camera until 1979. The word "Road" was not used after 1st May 1972. (K.W.Jones/D.Edge coll.)

Other views can be found in pictures 83-95
in *Hereford to Newport*
and nos 1-12 in
Pontypool to Mountain Ash.

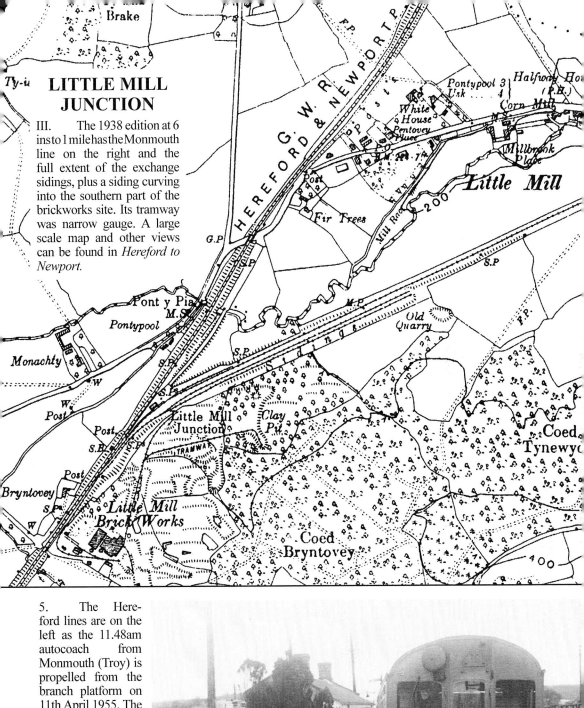

LITTLE MILL JUNCTION

III.   The 1938 edition at 6 ins to 1 mile has the Monmouth line on the right and the full extent of the exchange sidings, plus a siding curving into the southern part of the brickworks site. Its tramway was narrow gauge. A large scale map and other views can be found in *Hereford to Newport*.

5.   The Hereford lines are on the left as the 11.48am autocoach from Monmouth (Troy) is propelled from the branch platform on 11th April 1955. The station closed completely on 1st July 1863, but the branch platform was reopened on 1st May 1883. There had been a staff of 10 here in 1929. (R.M.Casserley)

6.　　The layout is seen from the signal box in 1961. The left siding crosses over the branch to provide a single public siding on which three wagons stand. Goods traffic ceased on 1st February 1965; all but one of the exchange sidings were lifted in 1964. (Stations UK)

7.　　A 1961 view towards the junction from the branch platform includes a northbound freight and a perforated signal arm, which was for shunting movements. The platform remained at this low height to the end; staffing ceased on 21st April 1952. (Stations UK)

8.   Coming off the branch on 8th May 1989 is no. 47330 with a train from the Royal Ordnance Factory at Glascoed. Such traffic continued until 31st January 1993 and the track was subsequently left in place. The signal box had been modernised in September 1979, when the number of levers was reduced from 55 to 17 and a panel was added. (P.G.Barnes)

GLASCOED

9.   This halt opened on the north side of the line on 23rd April 1938, as work was commencing on the Royal Ordnance Factory. The loop on the left was added at that time and it passed over the site of the first halt, which had opened on 16th May 1927. The local population in 1901 was only 215. (R.M.Casserley)

10.   A 1961 view from the bridge in the previous picture shows the line to the ROF still in use. The 61-lever signal box controlled access to the factory and was open from 21st August 1938 until 25th June 1962. Two lines diverged south from the loop and there were two platforms in the factory grounds. (Stations UK)

11.   The ROF platforms were recorded in the late 1960s, along with the centre engine release road. Trains brought workers in large numbers from Newport and the Monmouthshire Valleys from 12th December 1938. Platforms were provided in January 1939. (Lens of Sutton coll.)

12.   Glascoed Crossing Halt was ¼ mile east of the halt seen in pictures 9 and 10. The halt was also known as "West Access" and opened on 12th June 1941. The loop begins in the distance. (H.C.Casserley)

13.   A further ¾ mile east was Glascoed East Access Halt, which opened on 3rd February 1943, and this was on the south side of the line. This westward view is from 1955. The short-lived Wern Hir Halt was mid-way between here and West Access. None were for public use. (R.M.Casserley)

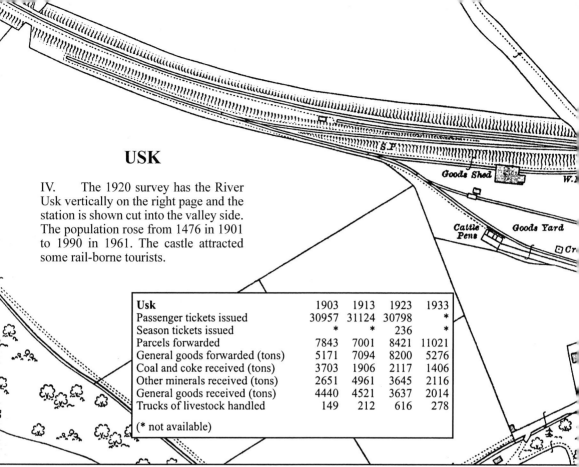

USK

IV.   The 1920 survey has the River Usk vertically on the right page and the station is shown cut into the valley side. The population rose from 1476 in 1901 to 1990 in 1961. The castle attracted some rail-borne tourists.

Usk	1903	1913	1923	1933
Passenger tickets issued	30957	31124	30798	*
Season tickets issued	*	*	236	*
Parcels forwarded	7843	7001	8421	11021
General goods forwarded (tons)	5171	7094	8200	5276
Coal and coke received (tons)	3703	1906	2117	1406
Other minerals received (tons)	2651	4961	3645	2116
General goods received (tons)	4440	4521	3637	2014
Trucks of livestock handled	149	212	616	278

(* not available)

14.   The staff pose in front of their creation in 1915. Twenty tons of stone were used in the rockery and creepers were trained to form the 7ft high letters. From 1923 to 1937 there were 8 or 9 men here, but in 1938 the figure rose to 30, as it included the railwaymen at Glascoed involved in the preparation for war. (GWR Magazine)

➔ 15. An LMS notice board is seen on the steps of the footbridge, which was dismantled in the late 1930s and never replaced. The tunnel was 256yds in length. All the buildings, including the signal box and goods shed, dated from 1893-97. (Stations UK)

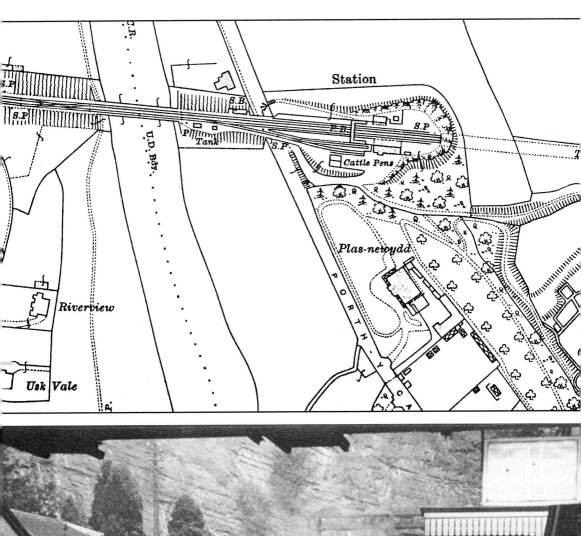

16.   The alternative to the footbridge can be seen as an autocoach arrives from Monmouth on 11th April 1955. One train from Pontypool Road terminated here at 8.47am in the 1940s and returned at 8.50. (R.M.Casserley)

17.   There was an engine shed and a small turntable on the right in the early years. Vans stand in Upper Yard; Lower Yard had a 5-ton crane. Both closed on 13th September 1965 and the branch was cut back to Glascoed. (D.K.Jones coll.)

18.   The 37-lever signal box closed in 1960 and is in the distance in this 1961 photograph. The end of the operational line had been at the tunnel mouth since June 1955; the track at the down platform had been lifted in 1959. (Stations UK)

CEFNTILLA HALT

19.   The halt was a late arrival, not opening until 14th June 1954. Two views from April 1955 reveal its unorthodox design, devoid of ramps. (H.C.Casserley)

20.   The stop was named after Cefntilla Court, an old manor house, as there was no village nearby. However, it attracted 300 passengers in some months, but had a life of less than one year. (R.M.Casserley)

LLANDENNY

Llandenny	1903	1913	1923	1933
Passenger tickets issued	9367	9335	10227	*
Season tickets issued	*	*	67	*
Parcels forwarded	347	682	891	984
General goods forwarded (tons)	1426	1553	2079	699
Coal and coke received (tons)	425	142	254	105
Other minerals received (tons)	864	2766	653	204
General goods received (tons)	337	517	406	171
Trucks of livestock handled	5	95	62	27

(* not available)

V. The station opened after the line, in October 1857. The population had reached only 322 by 1901. This extract is from 1920.

21. A 1936 southward photograph features the small signal box, which had a frame with eleven levers. It was in use until line closure, as was the goods yard. There was a staff of three for most of the 1930s. (Stations UK)

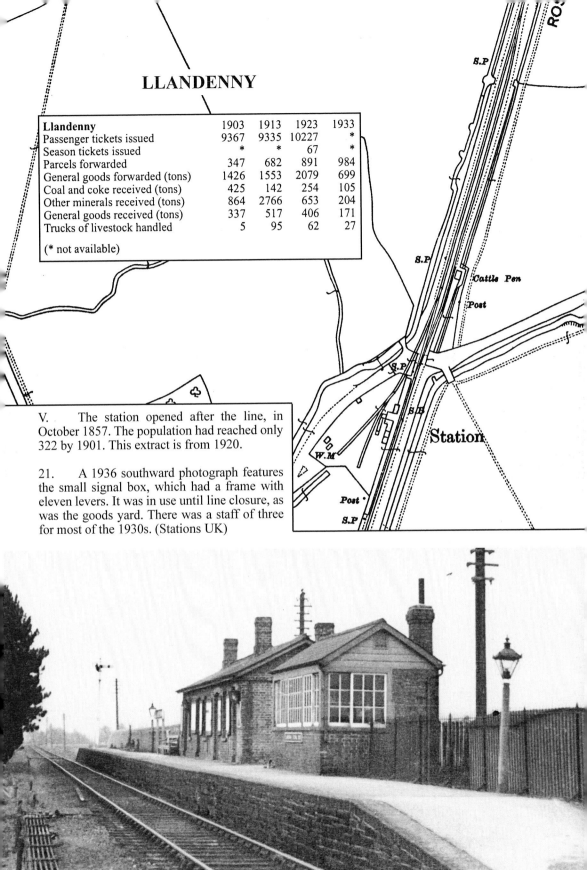

22.   Still looking south, we can examine the cattle pen and the goods loop, which could accommodate 22 wagons, but probably never did. The picture was taken only weeks before closure. (H.C.Casserley)

23.   Few stations changed so little as this one. The short siding near the weighing machine and loop lengthening were notable exceptions. A special ran over the closed line on 12th October 1957 and every detail was examined. (G.Adams/M.J.Stretton coll.)

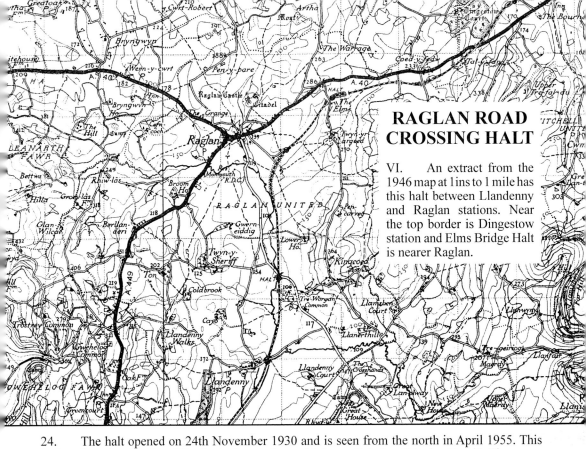

RAGLAN ROAD CROSSING HALT

VI.   An extract from the 1946 map at 1ins to 1 mile has this halt between Llandenny and Raglan stations. Near the top border is Dingestow station and Elms Bridge Halt is nearer Raglan.

24.   The halt opened on 24th November 1930 and is seen from the north in April 1955. This is thought to be the site of Raglan's first station, which was listed as "Raglan Road". There was another listed upon the opening of the line as "Raglan Footpath" and it was about one mile to the north. Both are assumed to have lasted until 1876. (R.M.Casserley)

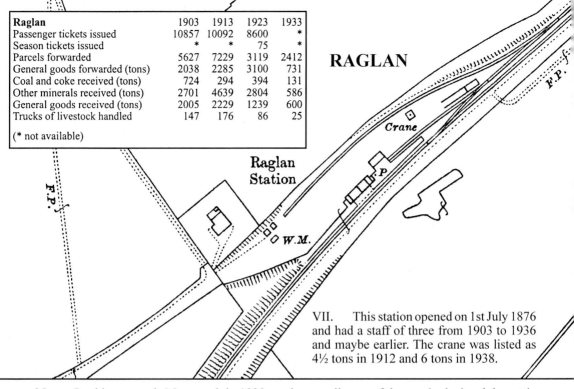

Raglan	1903	1913	1923	1933
Passenger tickets issued	10857	10092	8600	*
Season tickets issued	*	*	75	*
Parcels forwarded	5627	7229	3119	2412
General goods forwarded (tons)	2038	2285	3100	731
Coal and coke received (tons)	724	294	394	131
Other minerals received (tons)	2701	4639	2804	586
General goods received (tons)	2005	2229	1239	600
Trucks of livestock handled	147	176	86	25

(* not available)

RAGLAN

Crane

Raglan
Station

P

W.M.

F.P.

F.P.

VII.   This station opened on 1st July 1876
and had a staff of three from 1903 to 1936
and maybe earlier. The crane was listed as
4½ tons in 1912 and 6 tons in 1938.

25.   Looking towards Monmouth in 1939, we have a glimpse of the goods shed and the cattle
pen. The lighting was entirely by paraffin. (Stations UK)

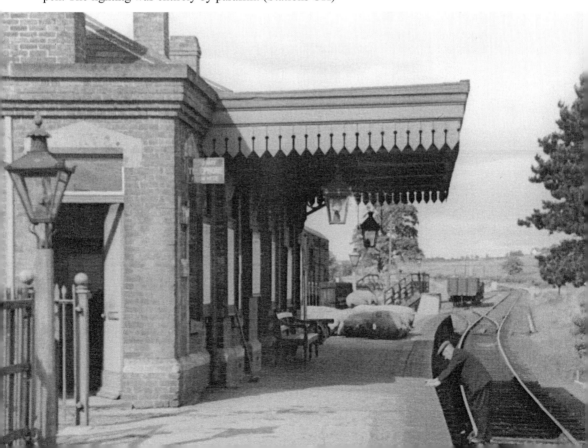

26.   A view in the other direction also includes the offer YOU MAY TELEPHONE FROM HERE. After the call, the operator would advise the clerk of the charge. The population rose from 619 in 1901 to 1222 in 1961. (H.C.Casserley)

27.   A second picture from April 1955 and this features the two-siding goods yard, which was in use until 13th June 1955 and later became a highways depot. The goods shed was dismantled and re-erected as a workshop at Norchard on the Dean Forest Railway, in 1992. (H.C.Casserley)

ELMS BRIDGE HALT

28.   The stop was in use from 27th November 1933 and was photographed three years after line closure. (M.Hale)

Dingestow	1903	1913	1923	1933
Passenger tickets issued	8143	6548	6742	*
Season tickets issued	*	*	41	*
Parcels forwarded	1380	1522	1211	1401
General goods forwarded (tons)	530	656	680	573
Coal and coke received (tons)	68	96	103	50
Other minerals received (tons)	740	3310	836	911
General goods received (tons)	419	532	307	176
Trucks of livestock handled	-	22	50	7

(* not available)

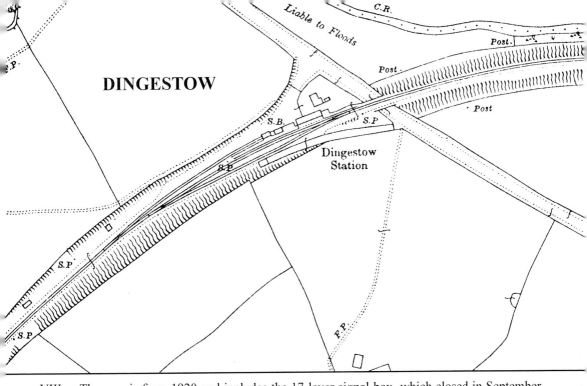

DINGESTOW

VIII.   The map is from 1920 and includes the 17-lever signal box, which closed in September 1931. The station was about half a mile from the village, which housed 196 souls in 1901. There was one man employed here after 1932.

29.   The SLS special was recorded on 12th October 1957, more than two years after the last passenger train had left. As at Raglan, goods services had lasted two weeks longer. On the right is the 1910 cattle dock. The "Usk-Monmouth Centenary" was hauled by 0-6-0PT no. 4668. (R.F.Roberts/Stephenson Locomotive Society coll.)

MONMOUTH (TROY)

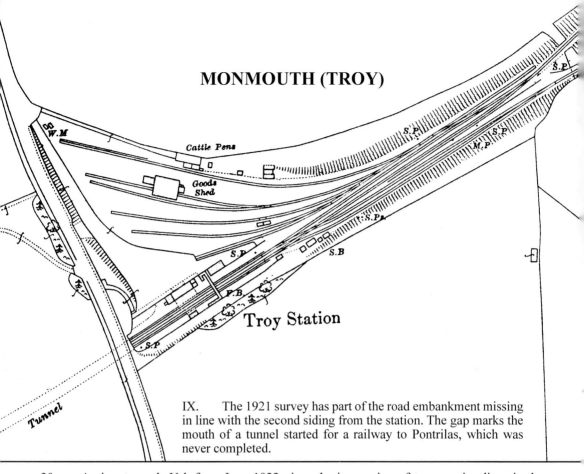

Cattle Pens

Goods Shed

Troy Station

Tunnel

IX.   The 1921 survey has part of the road embankment missing in line with the second siding from the station. The gap marks the mouth of a tunnel started for a railway to Pontrilas, which was never completed.

30.   A view towards Usk from June 1922 gives the impression of two running lines in the tunnel. However, the one on the left was only a siding. The tunnel was 148yds in length. (R.S.Carpenter coll.)

31.   The station had 18 to 21 employees in the 1930s, while the town had a population of 5000 to 5800 in 1900 to 1960. This view in the opposite direction is also from 1922. (R.S.Carpenter coll.)

32.   A panorama over the approach road in 1931 reveals the high proportion of privately owned wagons in that era. The match wagon was not for such commodities, but for use with cranes. (H.C.Casserley)

← 33. Railcars nos 23 and 30 were recorded on 16th September 1949. The platform on the left was used for terminating trains from Chepstow and also Ross-on-Wye.
(R.J.Buckley/M.Dart coll.)

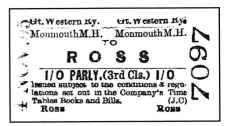

← 34. The vista from the footbridge in 1957 includes a railcar from Ross-on-Wye and an autotrain bound for it. Less obvious is a loco in the goods yard and the viaduct beyond the signal box. (R.A.Lumber)

35.   Taking water on 11th April 1955 is 0-4-2T no. 1421, which had propelled the two coaches from Chepstow, leaving at 10.40am. The footbridge had lost its roof by that date. (H.C.Casserley)

Monmouth (Troy)	1903	1913	1923	1933
Passenger tickets issued	48287	44122	32335	7599
Season tickets issued	*	*	45	60
Parcels forwarded	10422	17198	12551	34043
General goods forwarded (tons)	6087	8652	8864	5106
Coal and coke received (tons)	3243	3112	2583	1277
Other minerals received (tons)	4761	9733	8031	8513
General goods received (tons)	9492	10036	8890	8988
Trucks of livestock handled	544	787	954	416
(* not available)				

36.   An 0-6-0PT is departing for Chepstow and is climbing at 1 in 66 onto the viaduct. Almost parallel are the nearly level lines to Ross-on-Wye. (R.Holmes)

37.   The differing gradients are more obvious in this photograph from 22nd August 1958 of electric train staff exchange. The fireman of a train from Ross-on-Wye is surrendering it. The Chepstow route, on the right, was known as the Wye Valley Line. (E.Wilmshurst)

↓ 38. We look out of the west end of the tunnel in November 1958 at the disused line to Usk (right) and the siding (left). Near the van is a ground frame, the function of which was to lock the crane to prevent it swinging over the track during shunting movements. (J.Langford)

39.   This is the last day of passenger service - 3rd January 1959. On the right is the 11.00am from Ross-on-Wye, pushed by 0-4-2T no. 1455, and on the left is the 11.50 to Chepstow, which was worked by 0-6-0PT no. 7774. No. 7712 is just visible in the yard. The footbridge has gone. (H.Ballantyne)

Gt. Western Ry.   Gt. Western Ry.

BIGSWEIR   ro   BIGSWEIR

RAGLAN

Via Monmouth

1/O PARLY,(3rdCls.) 1/O

Issued subject to the conditions & regu-
lations set out in the Company's Time
Tables Books and Bills.   (O.G.)

Raglan   Ra n

40.   A 1961 picture shows the goods yard still busy; it closed on 6th January 1964. The massive modesty screens still stand on the left. The main building was dismantled in 1990 and later rebuilt at Winchcombe - see picture no. 81 in our *Stratford-upon-Avon to Cheltenham* album. The ticket office and the refreshment room both remained open for a while after the last passenger train had left. (Stations UK)

41.   Shunting on 14th April 1962 was 0-6-0PT no. 7403. All the signal arms had gone, as the signal box had closed on 27th March 1960, after which time it served as a ground frame working the points. The box had 38 levers. (C.G.Maggs)

EAST OF MONMOUTH (TROY)

42. The bridge over the River Wye for trains to Ross-on-Wye was photographed from a train bound for Chepstow in the snow on 4th January 1959. The structure is 99yds in length. (P.Kingston)

43. The other bridge and the viaduct for trains to Chepstow are seen in January 1959. All the structures were still standing in 2007. (D.Lawrence)

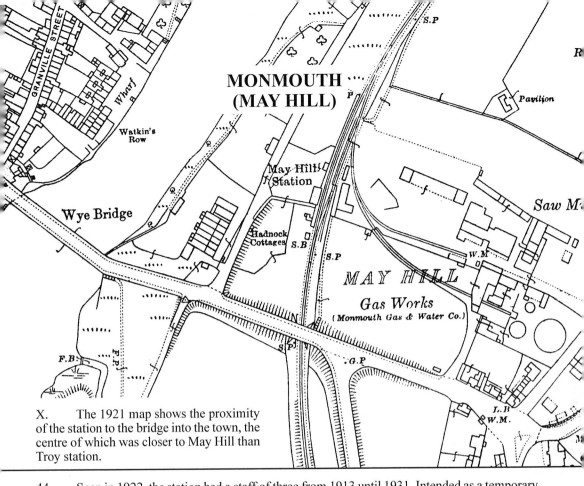

MONMOUTH (MAY HILL)

X. The 1921 map shows the proximity of the station to the bridge into the town, the centre of which was closer to May Hill than Troy station.

44. Seen in 1922, the station had a staff of three from 1913 until 1931. Intended as a temporary terminus, the station was retained as an experiment, which proved so successful that it was kept permanently and buildings were added by 1875. (R.S.Carpenter coll.)

45.   No. 1456 was bound for Ross-on-Wye on 24th July 1958 as the gate over the former loop was recorded. The connection here was removed in 1953, but the remainder of the line was usable until 1960. (G.Adams/M.J.Stretton coll.)

46.   The 15-lever signal box was in use from 1905 until January 1959, its predecessor being behind the camera. (R.K.Blencowe)

47.　　No. 1424 was propelling the 11.0am departure to Monmouth Troy on 1st November 1958. Most passengers destined for the town left the train here. (J.Langford)

48.　　A 1961 panorama includes part of the gasworks site and timber yard. Both had private sidings for many years, but there was no public goods traffic here. The town was gas lit from 1829, but the works here did not open until 1870. By 1900, it was consuming 1360 tons of coal per annum, this rising to 2381 in 1939 and over 4000 when the grid arrived in 1968. The cylinder was a high pressure storage vessel, which supplemented the traditional gas holder. The town's electricity works (1898-1937) demanded similar quantities of fuel by rail. Out of sight, there had been a siding laid in 1942 for a Ministry of Food store. (J.Langford)

HADNOCK HALT

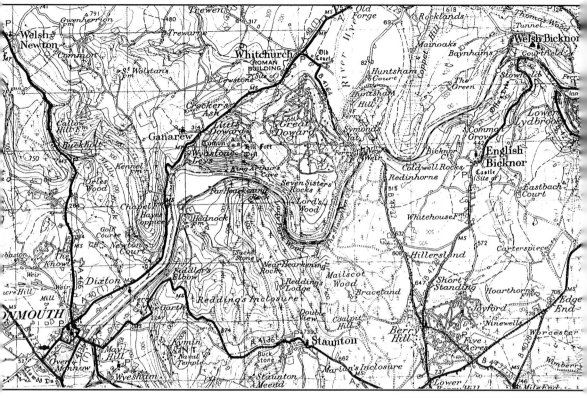

XI.   The halt is left of centre on this 1ins to 1 mile map published in 1952. Lydbrook Junction is top right.

49.   The halt opened on 7th May 1951 and was situated near the farm of that name. Hadnock Siding was ½ mile to the south and this opened on 13th July 1944; it was used mainly for loading timber from Reddings Inclosure. One mile north of the halt was Hadnock Quarry Siding, which was in use in 1922-55. (A.Dudman)

EAST OF HADNOCK HALT

50.   A further ¾ mile and one passed High Meadow Siding, where iron ore and iron oxide were loaded, also timber and coal, at different periods between 1873 and 1955. This 1922 southward view shows the loop from which the siding branched. It was known as Slaughter Siding at that time and there had earlier been a wharf nearby. (P.Rutherford/R.S.Carpenter coll.)

Monmouth (May Hill)	1903	1913	1923	1933
Passenger tickets issued	19696	17410	16551	5050
Season tickets issued	*	*	38	121
Parcels forwarded	31284	31147	30248	5007
(* not available)				

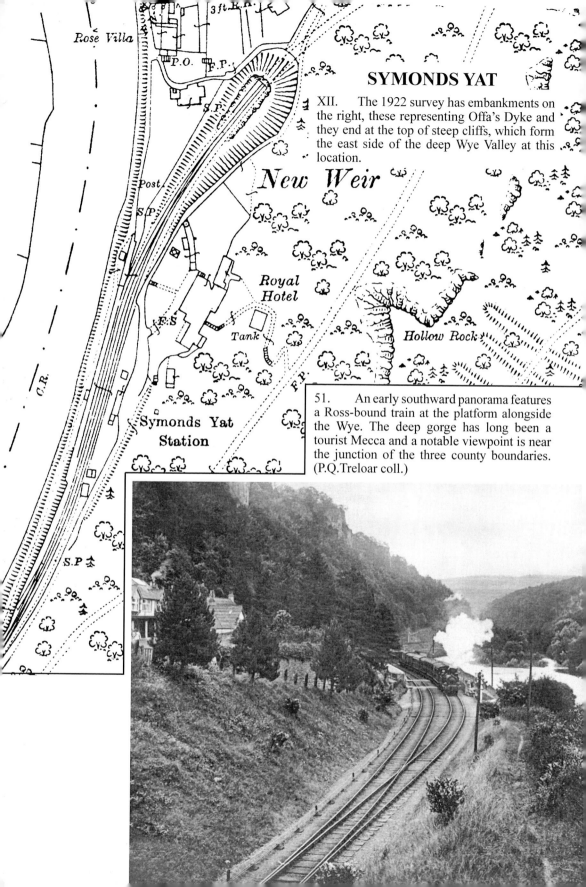

SYMONDS YAT

XII.   The 1922 survey has embankments on the right, these representing Offa's Dyke and they end at the top of steep cliffs, which form the east side of the deep Wye Valley at this location.

New Weir

Royal Hotel

Tank

Hollow Rock

Symonds Yat Station

51.   An early southward panorama features a Ross-bound train at the platform alongside the Wye. The deep gorge has long been a tourist Mecca and a notable viewpoint is near the junction of the three county boundaries. (P.Q.Treloar coll.)

Rose Villa

P.O.   F.P.

S.P.

Post

S.P.

F.S

C.R.

S.P

52.   The points in the foreground of picture 51 are seen again, the steep inclines being even more obvious. The rock is Carboniferous Limestone and the tunnel through it was 433yds in length. (R.S.Carpenter coll.)

53.   Four more pictures from 1922 complete our survey of this idyllic location in a peaceful era. There were seldom two passenger trains here, but a goods train was passed twice a day for many years. (R.S.Carpenter coll.)

54.   This was a fine location for visitor accommodation with views over the station. The signal box was in use from about 1902 until March 1953; the frame had eight levers. There was a staff of three in the 1930s. (R.S.Carpenter coll.)

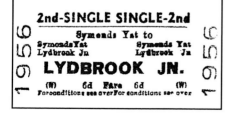

2nd-SINGLE SINGLE-2nd
Symonds Yat to
Symonds Yat   Symonds Yat
Lydbrook Jn   Lydbrook Jn
LYDBROOK   JN.
(W)   6d   Fare   6d   (W)
For conditions see over For conditions see over

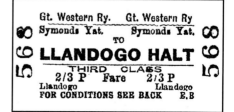

Gt. Western Ry.   Gt. Western Ry
Symonds Yat.   Symonds Yat.
                TO
LLANDOGO HALT
THIRD   CLASS
2/3 P   Fare   2/3 P
Llandogo   Llandogo
FOR CONDITIONS SEE BACK   E.B

55.	There was no footbridge to impede the view of the remarkable rock outcrops on the skyline. The small waiting shelter on the right was cantilevered out over the river bank. (R.S.Carpenter coll.)

56.	The loop was converted to a siding in March 1953 and a camping coach was sited on it for several Summers. No. 1455 simmers gently in about 1955. (Stephenson Locomotive Society coll.)

57. The headboard reads LAST TRAIN MONMOUTH-ROSS 4th JAN 1959. The special was run by the Stephenson Locomotive Society and started from Chepstow at 11.30am. On the other end of the eight coaches was 0-6-0PT no. 6439. (G.Adams/M.J.Stretton coll.)

58. Boarded up and neglected, the station was returning to nature in June 1963. The need for a modesty screen had long been forgotten. (T.Gough/M.J.Stretton coll.)

LYDBROOK JUNCTION

XIII.   The 1873 route from Ross to Monmouth is from top to bottom and on the right is the 1874 line from Lydney. The exchange sidings are on the lower part of the map. The sidings near the factory were for public goods traffic, but part of one was extended and designated a private siding in 1916.

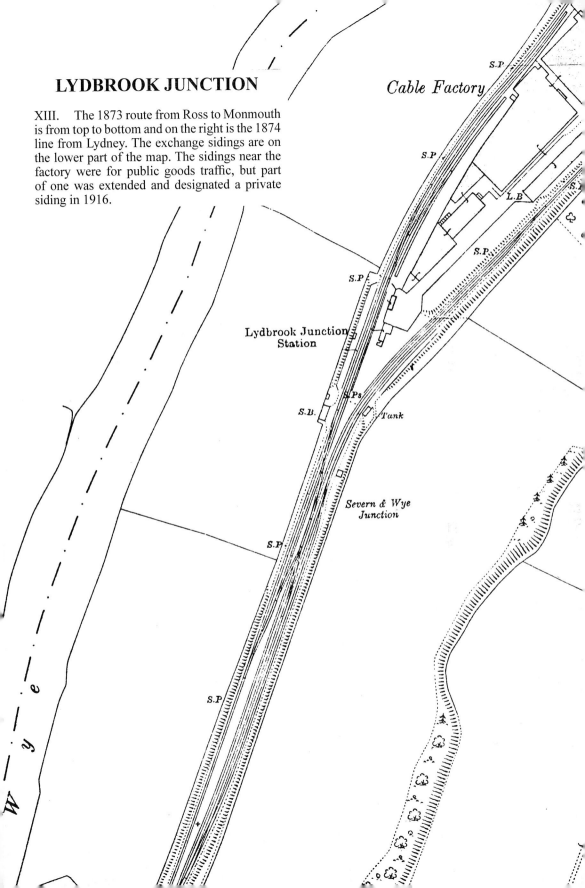

Cable Factory

S.P

S.P

L.B

S.P

S.P

S.P

Lydbrook Junction
Station

S.Ps

S.B.

Tank

*Severn & Wye
Junction*

S.P

S.P

W
y
e

59.   A train from Ross-on-Wye to Monmouth is signalled in this 1922 view. The Severn & Wye platform on the left had been little used. The signal box dated from 1908 and it had a massive 43-lever frame. (R.S.Carpenter coll.)

60.   The previous photograph was taken from near the centre of this one, which is from 1923. The suffix "Junction" was used from 1899 and some Midland Railway trains from Sharpness had terminated at this platform. (Stations UK)

↓ 61. No. 1401 gained fame in the film *The Titfield Thunderbolt* and is seen on 15th May 1957 arriving with the 3.51pm from Monmouth Troy. On the left is no. 9619 waiting to shunt the local goods. (H.Ballantyne)

62.   No details survive regarding this train, which is being propelled towards Monmouth. The number of employees increased from six to eight in the 1920s-30s, but passenger bookings remained fairly static at around 5000 per annum. (M.J.Stretton coll.)

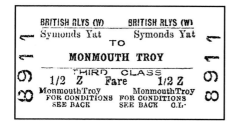

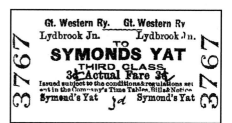

63.   In the background is the works of Edison Swan Cables, so called from 1926-1961, after which time it was AEI. This northward view is from 1961 and includes the rodding to the signal box, which closed on 26th February 1961. (Stations UK)

64.   The platform on the right had not been used by passengers since 8th July 1929 and the Nissen hut had been erected on it during World War II. The other platforms had been idle since 1959, but freight continued this far until 2nd November 1964. AEI retained its siding until 31st October 1965. The lines on the right were used as sidings after 1956. (Lens of Sutton coll.)

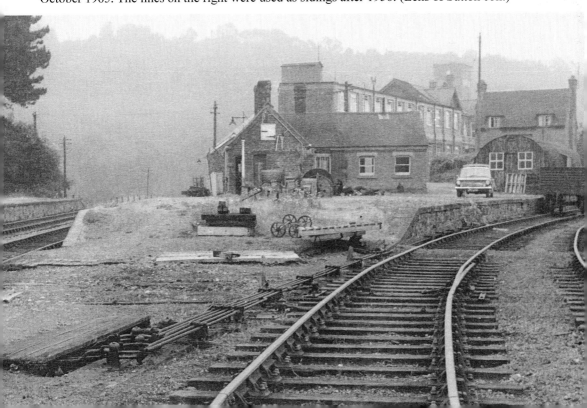

2. Coleford Branch

NEWLAND

Cherry Orchard

Spout

Newland
Station

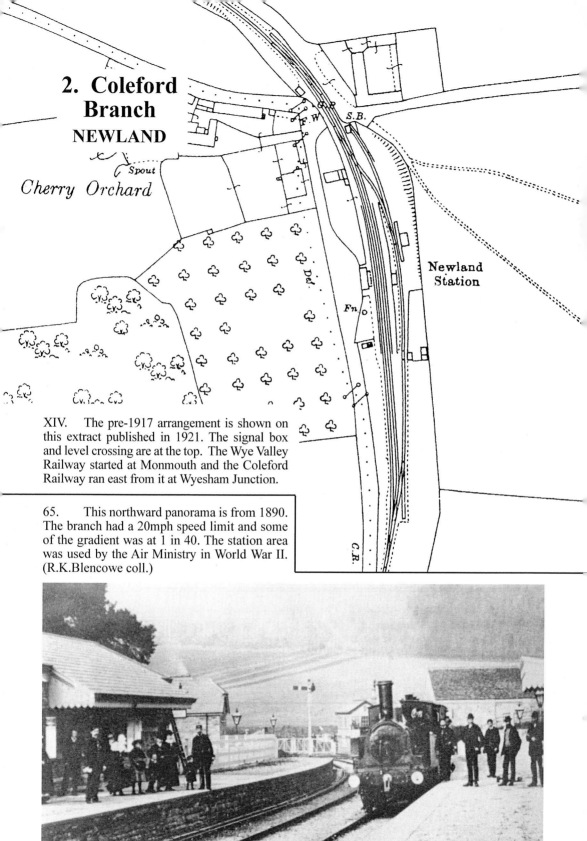

XIV. The pre-1917 arrangement is shown on this extract published in 1921. The signal box and level crossing are at the top. The Wye Valley Railway started at Monmouth and the Coleford Railway ran east from it at Wyesham Junction.

65. This northward panorama is from 1890. The branch had a 20mph speed limit and some of the gradient was at 1 in 40. The station area was used by the Air Ministry in World War II. (R.K.Blencowe coll.)

66.   The branch opened on 1st September 1883 and this was the only intermediate station. The line closed on 1st January 1917 and the rails were taken up for Army use in World War I, never to be relaid. This westward view is from about 1923. (Stations UK)

67.   Looking towards Coleford, we see level land in the distance, where the loop ended and a goods loop joined. This extended behind the shelter on the left and ran near a small goods shed. There were the two Redbrook Tunnels west of the station (264yds and 66yds) and the 278yd Newland Tunnel was east thereof. (Lens of Sutton coll.)

WEST OF COLEFORD

68.   About one mile of track west of Coleford was not lifted in 1917, but was retained to serve Whitecliff Quarry. A variety of businesses had private siding agreements from October 1885 until May 1967. Timber, lime and limestone were loaded here. Ex-GWR 0-6-0PT no. 1623 takes water on 16th December 1961. (R.Denison)

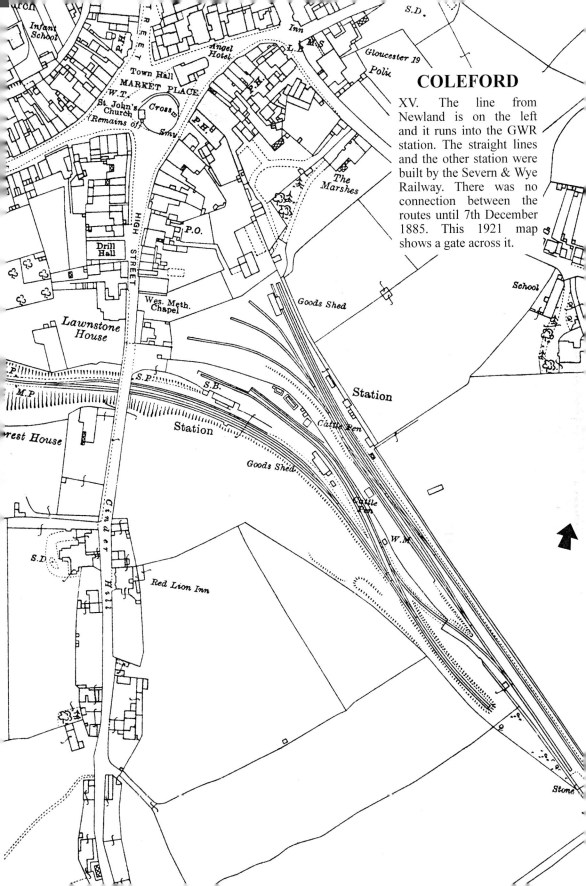

COLEFORD

XV. The line from Newland is on the left and it runs into the GWR station. The straight lines and the other station were built by the Severn & Wye Railway. There was no connection between the routes until 7th December 1885. This 1921 map shows a gate across it.

Infant School

P.H.

Town Hall

MARKET PLACE

Angel Hotel

Inn

L.B.

M.S.

Gloucester 19

Poli.

W.T.

St. John's Church (Remains of)

Cross

Smy.

P.H.

P.H.

The Marshes

School

Drill Hall

HIGH STREET

P.O.

Wes. Meth. Chapel

Goods Shed

Lawnstone House

S.P.

S.P.

S.B.

Station

M.P.

M.P.

Station

Cattle Pen

rest House

Goods Shed

Cattle Pen

Cinder Hill

S.D.

Red Lion Inn

W.M.

Stone

69.   An Edwardian postcard featured the GWR station and signal box, both of which ceased to be used on the last day of 1916. (Stations UK)

Other views of this station can be seen in pictures 82 to 87 in *Branch Lines around Lydney*.

70.   This is a rare shot of a Monmouth train at Coleford before 1917. Roses and guidance for gentlemen seem to have been top priority in this period. (M.Dart coll.)

71.   The features noted in the last caption had gone when this photograph was taken in June 1922. Gentlemen were generally abiding by the law by that time, although there was a legal provision regarding cart wheels of the type seen and the need to moisten the hubs in dry weather. (R.S.Carpenter coll.)

72.   Little had changed by 23rd September 1950, when ex-GWR railcar no. W1 was recorded on a Birmingham Railway Society railtour. Regular passenger service had been withdrawn on 8th July 1929. The S&WR station is in the right background. (Stephenson Locomotive Society coll.)

73. The layout was simplified in 1951 to give a direct link between the two routes. Most goods yards received a sectional concrete warehouse for agricultural commodities in the mid-1950s. This is a 1961 panorama. (J.Langford)

74. No. 4624 runs through the former Monmouth platform on 17th December 1963 with ballast from Whitecliff Quarry. Morris Minors were spreading everywhere by that time. (M.A.N.Johnston)

75.   The Railway Enthusiasts Club ran a special train to Whitecliff Quarry on 20th June 1964, using 0-6-0PTs nos. 1658 and 1644. Diesel traction on stone trains began with the first trip in 1966. The goods yard closed on 1st August 1967. (R.K.Blencowe)

76.   The goods shed was transformed into Coleford Railway Museum in 1988 and Peckett 0-4-0ST no. 1893 of 1936 is seen in September 1995, having spent its working life at power stations. Brought to the site in 1987 was the signal box from Cogload Junction, near Taunton, and in it was fitted the frame from Shelwick Junction, near Hereford. (M.Dart)

3. Wye Valley Branch
WYESHAM HALT

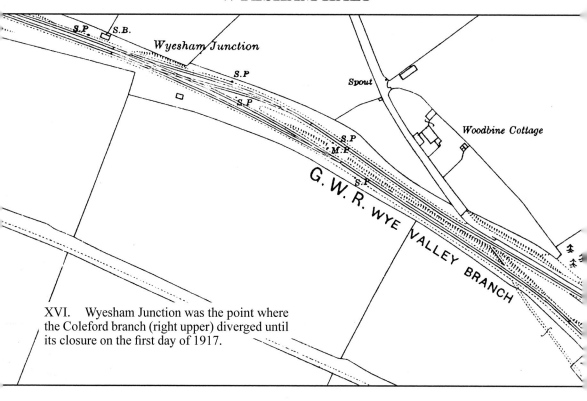

XVI. Wyesham Junction was the point where the Coleford branch (right upper) diverged until its closure on the first day of 1917.

77. The halt was built a little to the north of the site of the junction and was opened on 12th January 1931, on the south side of the line. (Stations UK)

78.　　The girders of the bridge over the A466 are included in this view towards Monmouth from July 1959. All these features have vanished. Pupils for Monmouth Boys School alighted here, while the girls continued to Monmouth (Troy) station. (H.C.Casserley)

REDBROOK-ON-WYE

XVII. The 1922 edition includes the crane, which was rated at 5 tons. The viaduct commences near the lower border.

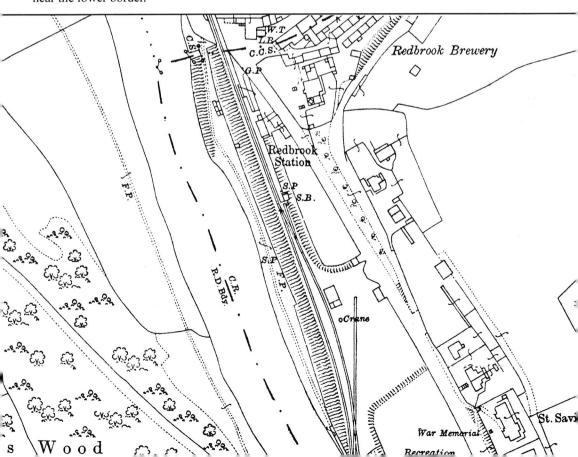

79.   The viaduct was 101yds long and was at the south end of the station, which is beyond the left border of this postcard. A rule dated 15th May 1926 allowed barrels for the Boat Inn to be unloaded at the far end of the bridge. There is a parallel footbridge, which is still in use. (Postcard)

→ 80. Another postcard features what appears to be a ground frame which has no rodding. The station master had two porters for most of the period between the wars. Moderate quantities of tinplate were produced nearby until 1961. (C.G.Maggs coll.)

Redbrook	1903	1913	1923	1933
Passenger tickets issued	7296	7560	7714	*
Season tickets issued	*	*	7	*
Parcels forwarded	1521	1706	1857	1491
General goods forwarded (tons)	3656	4063	3031	3197
Coal and coke received (tons)	252	626	1237	2469
Other minerals received (tons)	2418	4105	3654	4885
General goods received (tons)	3826	2492	788	*
Trucks of livestock handled	-	-	-	-
(* not available)				

→ 81. Looking towards the viaduct in June 1922, we see much of the goods yard, which was in use until 6th January 1964. The nearby brook was red due to iron oxide, which is still mined in the area as a pigment. (R.S.Carpenter coll.)

82. The proximity of the Wye is clear in this panorama from April 1955, when fine vistas were protected from tree growth. The signal box was opened only during shunting; it had ten levers. The suffix had been added to the place name on 11th September 1933. The site was cleared to make way for a restaurant. (H.C.Casserley)

83. The public footbridge is seen from a train departing south for Chepstow on 15th September 1956. The points to the goods yard are included. (R.M.Casserley)

PENALLT HALT

84.   Seen on 11th September 1953 is the structure which came into use on 3rd August 1931. It was nearer to Redbrook Viaduct than Redbrook itself. The justification for two stops so close together was the presence of the river. This is a northward view. (Lens of Sutton coll.)

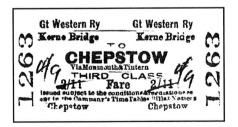

WHITEBROOK HALT

85.   We look towards Monmouth from the driving compartment on 11th April 1955. This stop opened on 1st February 1927 and was 1¾ miles from Penallt Halt. (H.C.Casserley)

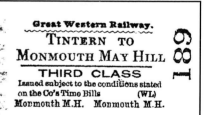

St. Briavels	1903	1913	1923	1933
Passenger tickets issued	8587	8890	9171	*
Season tickets issued	*	*	45	*
Parcels forwarded	4319	6307	5958	5638
General goods forwarded (tons)	1999	2068	3895	400
Coal and coke received (tons)	132	73	104	53
Other minerals received (tons)	149	254	719	205
General goods received (tons)	859	1051	1043	563
Trucks of livestock handled	-	66	23	8

(* not available)

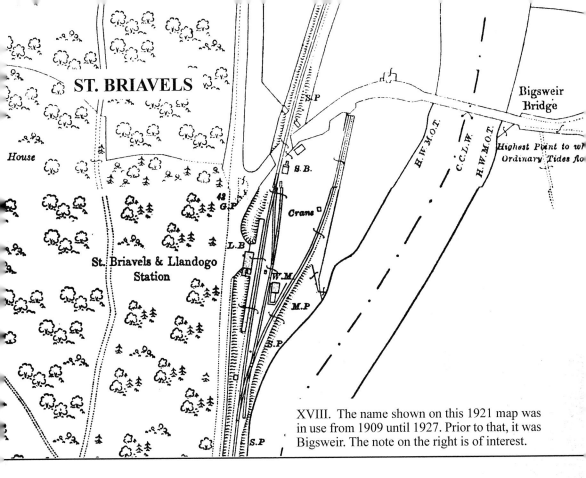

ST. BRIAVELS

Bigsweir Bridge

House

S.P

S.B.

43
G.P

Crane

L.B

St. Briavels & Llandogo
Station

W.M

M.P

S.P

H.W.M.O.T.

C.C.L.W.

H.W.M.O.T.

Highest Point to wʰ
Ordinary Tides flo

S.P

XVIII. The name shown on this 1921 map was
in use from 1909 until 1927. Prior to that, it was
Bigsweir. The note on the right is of interest.

86.   This northward panorama is from June 1922 and includes a combined road and rail vehicle
weigh bridge. It was fine for a single axle cart. There was usually a staff of two serving the local
population, which numbered a little over 1000 in 1900-60. Freight traffic ceased on 5th January
1959. (R.S.Carpenter coll.)

87.   The 15-lever signal box served as a ground frame from November 1928 to February 1959. The fireman of this down stone train on 14th April 1962 is opening the gates himself. Improvements to the A466 have altered this view totally. (C.G.Maggs)

LLANDOGO HALT

88.   This facility was available from 9th March 1927 and is seen in September 1956. Note the hook for a lamp on winter evenings and the step for short guards to reach it. (R.M.Casserley)

BROCKWEIR HALT

89.   No. 6426 is calling on 18th October 1958, while bound for Chepstow. The halt opened on 19th August 1929. The village was accessed by a bridge over the river, built in 1904. It was earlier the highest point on the river for many ships. (S.Rickard/J&J coll.)

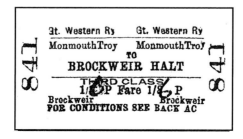

TINTERN

XIX.   At the bottom of this 1921 map is the
182yd long Tintern Tunnel and south of it was
the junction for the Tintern Wireworks siding.
Part of this line is lower left; the ruins of Tintern
Abbey stand south of it.

Tintern	1903	1913	1923	1933
Passenger tickets issued	18292	18746	18831	*
Season tickets issued	*	*	91	*
Parcels forwarded	4777	9501	7110	8056
General goods forwarded (tons)	1594	3047	6173	*
Coal and coke received (tons)	301	112	154	*
Other minerals received (tons)	447	442	368	*
General goods received (tons)	1293	1530	1593	*
Trucks of livestock handled	11	33	36	*

(* not available)

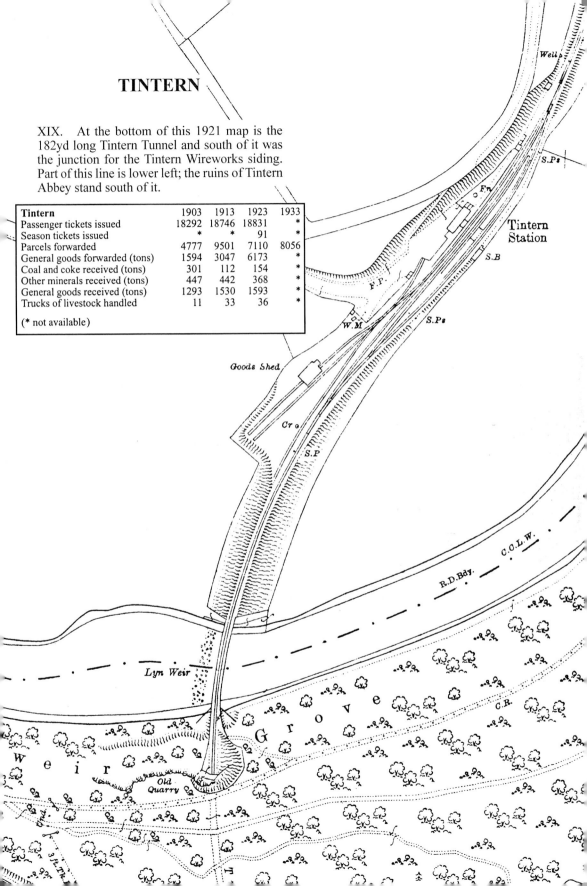

90.   A panorama from between the wars includes a bus as a reminder of the reason for the downfall of passenger numbers. The staff was reduced from five to four in that period. (Postcard)

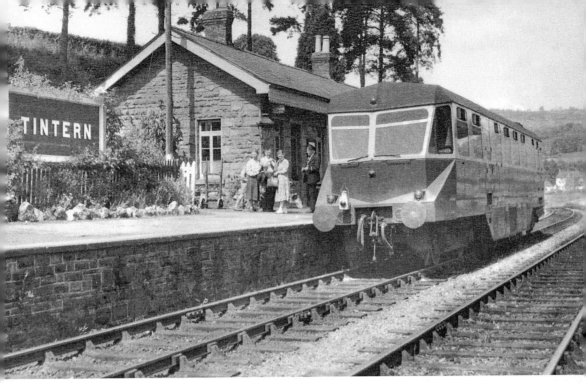

91.   Railcar no. W30 was one of a batch built in 1941-42 and is seen working the 2.40pm Chepstow to Monmouth service on 21st June 1951, when the floral displays were at their peak. (Stephenson Locomotive Society coll.)

92.   This photograph was taken on 11th April 1955, from the front of the Monmouth-bound train seen in the next picture. The crane (left) was rated at six tons. Tintern had a population of 641 in 1961. (H.C.Casserley)

93. This was the only passing place on the route and the platform on the left had two faces. The signal box was usable until 27th March 1960; there were 25 levers in it. (H.C.Casserley)

94. A northward view from 1956 reveals signalling that allowed only goods trains to depart north from the outer face of the island platform. The large nameboard showed TINTERN FOR BROCKWEIR until 1929. (R.M.Casserley)

95.   The last passenger train to traverse the route was recorded through countless lenses on 4th January 1959. No. 6439 was on the other end. Long excursion trains to this location had been common in the past. The goods yard was in use until 6th January 1964. (D.K.Jones coll.)

96.   Gwent County Council began restoring the station and signal box for tourist purposes in 1985. This stock was at the dock in April 2007 and in commercial use by Monmouthshire County Council. The area was heavily overgrown with trees and bore no resemblance to the views from the railway era. (B.D.Mitchell)

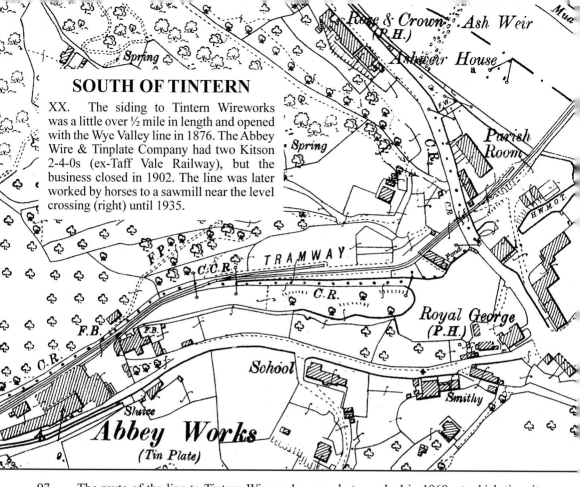

SOUTH OF TINTERN

XX.   The siding to Tintern Wireworks was a little over ½ mile in length and opened with the Wye Valley line in 1876. The Abbey Wire & Tinplate Company had two Kitson 2-4-0s (ex-Taff Vale Railway), but the business closed in 1902. The line was later worked by horses to a sawmill near the level crossing (right) until 1935.

97.   The route of the line to Tintern Wireworks was photographed in 1969, at which time it carried a roadway. (C.G.Maggs)

98. Brass was made in this vicinity from 1566 and it was probably the first place to have such a foundry. There was also a tannery and paper mills. The bridge (top right on map XX) now carries a public footpath, the track having been lifted in 1941. The structure is 69yds long and was photographed in 1993. (M.Dart)

99. Tintern Tunnel's north portal was recorded from the 69yd-long bridge over the River Wye on 26th June 1964. (M.A.N.Johnston)

100.   A southward view on the same day features the sidings opened by Tintern Quarries Ltd in 1931. Two other firms ran the quarry later and rail traffic ceased in 1986. There had been a staff halt on the left from 1931 until about 1949. It was 2½ miles from Wye Valley Junction. (M.A.N.Johnston)

NETHERHOPE HALT

101.   Tidenham Tunnel is in the background of this photograph from April 1955, taken from an autocoach destined for Monmouth. The bore was 1190ft in length. The halt had opened on 16th May 1932. (H.C.Casserley)

102.   Standing at the halt on 18th October is 0-6-0PT no. 6417. The access path handrails can be seen above the dome. (D.K.Jones coll.)

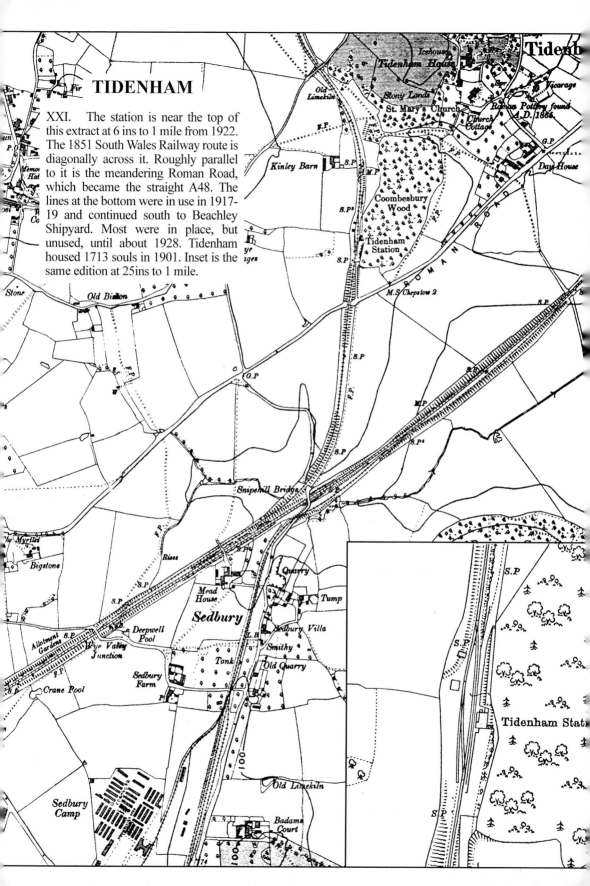

TIDENHAM

XXI. The station is near the top of this extract at 6 ins to 1 mile from 1922. The 1851 South Wales Railway route is diagonally across it. Roughly parallel to it is the meandering Roman Road, which became the straight A48. The lines at the bottom were in use in 1917-19 and continued south to Beachley Shipyard. Most were in place, but unused, until about 1928. Tidenham housed 1713 souls in 1901. Inset is the same edition at 25ins to 1 mile.

103.   An April 1955 northward view shows the site of the single siding, which was used until 7th February 1955. The station had been unstaffed since November 1952 and was closed from 1st January 1917 until 1st February 1918. The goods shed (left) housed a 30 cwt crane. (H.C.Casserley)

104.   There had been a special to Dayhouse Quarry on 13th August 1978. "Severnsider 2" is at that location on 30th June 1985, hauled by no. 20022. The quarry loop was relaid further north in 1968, the new one extending more than one mile from Wye Valley Junction. Traffic ceased on 29th March 1990. (D.H.Mitchell)

WYE VALLEY JUNCTION

105.   The junction is shown on the left side of the last map and we have three westward views from the road bridge. A Monmouth-Newport service is hauled by 0-4-2T no. 1421 on 21st May 1958 as the fireman surrenders the staff. (S.Rickard/J&J coll.)

Tidenham	1903	1913	1923	1933
Passenger tickets issued	6914	6160	7118	*
Season tickets issued	*	*	35	*
Parcels forwarded	2062	1311	816	799
General goods forwarded (tons)	392	552	762	*
Coal and coke received (tons)	165	91	71	*
Other minerals received (tons)	380	742	511	*
General goods received (tons)	740	738	592	*
(* not available)				

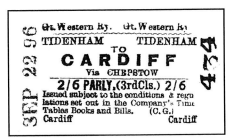

106.   Collecting the staff on the same day is one of the crew of 0-6-0PT no. 7764. Wye Valley Junction box was fitted with a 25-lever frame and functioned from 1875 to 1969. (S.Rickard/J&J coll.)

107. The junction was photographed in June 1979 and evident are the catch points which lead into a sand drag. This was provided for any runaways on the severe gradient of 1 in 66. (C.G.Maggs)

TUTSHILL HALT

➜ 108. These two pictures were taken from the west side of the bridge at Wye Valley Junction in 1958. Passing the down platform is 0-6-0PT no. 7754. (S.Rickard/ J&J coll.)

➜ 109. The halt opened on 9th July 1934 and was in use until Wye Valley services were withdrawn. The line descends in the distance at 1 in 100 towards Chepstow Bridge. (Stations UK)

EAST OF CHEPSTOW

110.   The first of Brunel's mighty wrought iron spans across the Wye gorge came into use on 19th July 1852 and the temporary Chepstow East station was then closed. The second span came into use on 18th April 1853. They are seen from the south. (R.Taylor)

111.   The bridge is viewed from the deep cutting on the east bank in April 1962. Work was about to start on replacement with lattice steel structures. The smaller spans at the other end had been changed in 1948. (C.G.Maggs)

➜ 112. A view from the west bank shows how the decks spring from the top of the limestone cliff. The tubular suspension spans were supported on cast iron cylinders filled with concrete and founded on rock 40ft down. (P.J.Kelley)

↘ 113. The replacement structures were built on the west bank and rolled under the original spans in 1962. This is the future support for the up line. The headroom requirements for shipping had been reduced with the abandonment of sail for commercial purposes. (C.G.Maggs coll.)

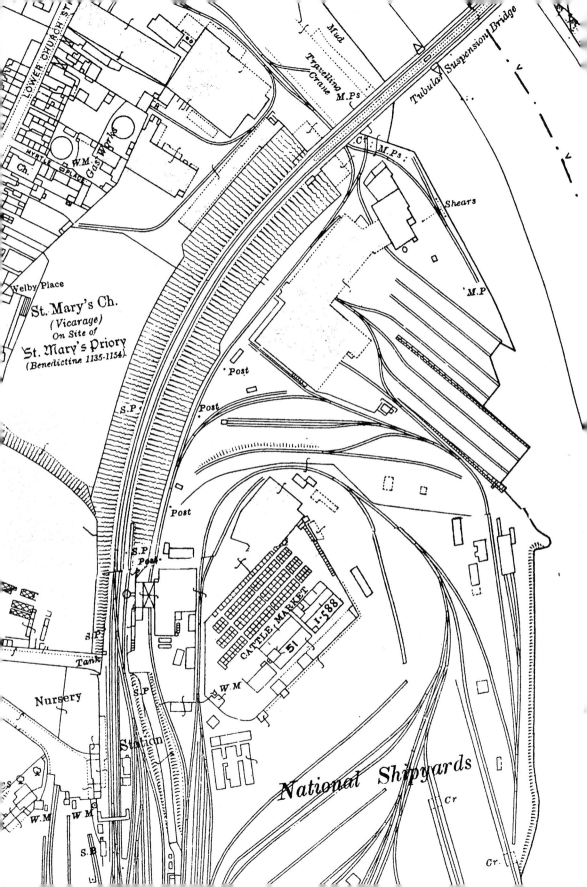

LOWER CHURCH ST.

Mud

Travelling Crane
M.Ps.

Tubular Suspension Bridge

MYRTLE PLACE Gas Works

W.M.

Ch.

C. M.Ps.

Shears

M.P.

Welby Place

St. Mary's Ch.
(Vicarage)
On Site of
St. Mary's Priory
(Benedictine 1135-1154)

Post

Post

S.P.

Post

Post

S.P.
Post

CATTLE MARKET

1·588

51

W.M

S.P.

Tank

Nursery

S.P.

Station

National Shipyards

Cr

W.M

W.M

Cr

S.B.

CHEPSTOW

← XXII. The bridge is at the top of this 1921 extract and the main line climbs steeply to it from the station, while the adjacent goods line drops down to the wharves and passes under the main tracks.

> **Other views of the main line can be found in pictures 51-62 in our *Gloucester to Cardiff* album.**

114. A 1953 photograph from the up platform features the down island. Monmouth trains generally used the far side of it, which was numbered 3, if they were terminating. However, most ran to Severn Tunnel Junction or Newport in later years. (Lens of Sutton coll.)

115.   If running from the west, the Monmouth train would use platform 1, as witnessed on 11th April 1955. No. 1421 will depart at 10.40am, propelling the train north. (H.C.Casserley)

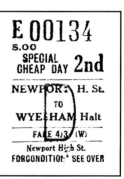

116.   The chalet style building was employed widely by Brunel on the many lines for which he was engineer. The prospective passenger's perspective was recorded in the mid-1960s; little had changed 40 years later, when it had been listed Grade II. (Lens of Sutton coll.)

117.   This June 1964 panorama has the option to change here painted out. The main building had been subjected to a noteworthy repositioning in 1877-78; it had been raised bodily 22ins. (R.G.Nelson coll./T.Walsh)

118.   The single line down to the wharves passed through the middle floor of the 1851 Steam Flour Mill (right). It was used as maltings in 1892-1926 and suffered a fire in 2002. A "Western" diesel hydraulic has its empty coal train on part of the bridge. (Lens of Sutton coll.)

↗ 119.   In the background is no. 4657 waiting to leave for Tintern Quarry with six empty hoppers and a brake van, on 24th April 1964. The signal box had 55 levers and functioned until 3rd March 1969. (M.A.N.Johnston)

→   120.   Our final view includes stone as a reminder of this once important traffic in the Wye Valley. The photograph is from July 1968; the goods yard closed nine months later, but passenger traffic is still healthy today. (R.Leleux/M.J.Stretton coll.)

PASSENGERS ARE
REQUESTED TO CROSS
THE LINE BY MEANS
OF THE BRIDGE

PASSENGERS ARE
REQUESTED TO CROSS
THE LINE BY MEANS
OF THE BRIDGE

MP Middleton Press

EVOLVING THE ULTIMATE RAIL ENCYCLOPEDIA

Easebourne Lane, Midhurst, West Sussex. GU29 9AZ   Tel:01730 813169

www.middletonpress.co.uk   email:info@middletonpress.co.uk

A-978 0 906520   B-978 1 873793   C-978 1 901706   D-978 1 904474
E-978 1 906008   F-978 1 908174

All titles listed below were in print at time of publication - please check current availability by looking at our website - *www.middletonpress.co.uk* or by requesting a Brochure which includes our *LATEST* RAILWAY TITLES also our TRAMWAY, TROLLEYBUS, MILITARY and COASTAL series